W9-BFC-087

REVOLUTIONARY DISCOVERIES OF SCIENTIFIC PIONEERS™

THE BIG BANG THEORY: EDWIN HUBBLE AND THE ORIGINS OF THE UNIVERSE

FRED BORTZ

ROSEN
PUBLISHING®

New York

Published in 2014 by The Rosen Publishing Group, Inc.
29 East 21st Street, New York, NY 10010

Library of Congress Cataloging-in-Publication Data

Bortz, Fred, 1944– author.
The big bang theory: Edwin Hubble and the origins of the universe/Fred Bortz.—First edition.
     pages cm.—(Revolutionary discoveries of scientific pioneers)
Includes bibliographical references and index.
ISBN 978-1-4777-1803-2 (library binding)
1. Hubble, Edwin Powell, 1889–1953—Juvenile literature. 2. Astronomers—United States—Biography—Juvenile literature. 3. Galaxies—Juvenile literature. 4. Expanding universe—Juvenile literature. I. Title.
QB36.H83B67 2014
523.1'8—dc23
                                                                              2013011361

Manufactured in the United States of America

CPSIA Compliance Information: Batch #W14YA: For further information, contact Rosen Publishing, New York, New York, at 1-800-237-9932.

A portion of the material in this book has been derived from *Hubble and the Big Bang* by Paul Kupperberg.

CONTENTS

INTRODUCTION

This is a book about the biggest subject you can imagine: the whole universe, and how humanity's ideas about the universe have changed. It is also about a person whose discovery extended the limits of the universe far beyond what others had imagined. In the late 1920s, he not only discovered the farthest reaches of space, but also, much to the astonishment of scientists everywhere, found clues to the beginning of time. That person was American scientist Edwin Powell Hubble, whose work transformed the field of science known as cosmology, the study of the origins, history, and future of the universe.

Although Hubble's revolutionary discovery transformed science's view of Earth's place in space, it was hardly the first such revolution. Humanity's view of the universe had changed dramatically many times since the earliest humans looked to the sky. To them, everything seemed obvious. An unmoving world was at the center of everything, and the sun, moon, planets, and stars circled around it, each following its own path.

In the sixteenth century, the first great revolution challenged that view of the universe. Nicolaus Copernicus placed the sun at the center, added Earth to the planets in orbit around the sun, and set it spinning on its axis. In the early seventeenth century, Johannes Kepler did calculations that showed that the orbits of

Hubble eXtreme Deep Field
HST ACS/WFC WFC3/IR
Lookback Time

Less than
5 billion years

5 billion to
9 billion years

More than
9 billion years

ASTRONOMER EDWIN HUBBLE'S DISCOVERIES ABOUT GALAXIES DRAMATICALLY CHANGED OUR UNDERSTANDING OF THE SIZE OF THE UNIVERSE AND ITS HISTORY. IN TRIBUTE TO THAT REVOLUTIONARY WORK, NASA NAMED THE HUBBLE SPACE TELESCOPE (HST) AFTER HIM. SINCE ITS LAUNCH IN 1990, THE HST HAS PRODUCED IMAGES THAT HAVE LED TO DISCOVERIES AS REMARKABLE AS THE ONES MADE BY HUBBLE HIMSELF. THE HUBBLE EXTREME DEEP FIELD IS A LOOK SO FAR INTO SPACE THAT IT SHOWS GALAXIES FROM A TIME WHEN THE UNIVERSE WAS LESS THAN A TENTH OF ITS CURRENT AGE.

planets were not perfect circles. He found three mathematical laws to describe their motion. At around the same time, Galileo Galilei made observations with his telescopes that showed that planets were other worlds. And late in that century, Sir Isaac Newton discovered the laws of motion and gravity that explained why Kepler's formulas had the mathematical form that they did.

None of those revolutionaries moved the sun from the center of everything, but by the mid-nineteenth century, astronomers realized that the sun was just one of many stars. Then in 1905, another revolution in cosmology began when Albert Einstein announced a groundbreaking theory of space and time. He stated that the position and motion of any body can be measured only in relation to another body and not in relation to any particular point. No point in the universe is special; that means it has no center at all. Ten years later, he extended that theory to explain gravity—yet another revolutionary idea. His mathematics was brilliant, but it required one peculiar quantity called the cosmological constant. Despite the success of his theory of relativity, Einstein found the need for that constant troublesome.

Then along came Hubble. His discoveries revealed a universe that was not only millions of times larger than people had ever before imagined, but one that was also expanding like a balloon. Einstein even thought that Hubble's findings solved the problem of the cosmological constant.

The latest astronomical observations show that Einstein was probably wrong to jump to that conclusion. Those discoveries have set in motion yet another revolution in cosmology. It is too soon to know where that revolution will lead, but it is not too soon to say that whatever path it takes will be grounded in the legacy of Edwin Powell Hubble.

CHAPTER ONE

THE MAKING OF A YOUNG ASTRONOMER

When Edwin Hubble was born in Marshfield, Missouri, on November 20, 1889, no one could have imagined that he would grow up to transform a field of science. But it did not take long for his interest in astronomy to become obvious to everyone. Edwin's grandfather, William Henderson James of Springfield, Missouri, owned a small telescope that he kept set up in his backyard. During a summer visit in 1897, Edwin spent hours in the evenings peering through the amazing device, watching the progress of celestial objects as they moved across the night sky. He was so fascinated by what he saw that he had only one present in mind for his upcoming eighth birthday: to spend the entire night, from dusk to dawn, observing the heavens through the lens of his grandfather's telescope.

GENTLEMEM
OUR
COUNTRY

HUBBLE LIVED IN A TIME OF GREAT TECHNOLOGICAL CHANGE. IN 1896, THE YEAR HE TURNED SEVEN YEARS OLD, HENRY FORD *(ABOVE)* BUILT THE FIRST AMERICAN CAR. THIS PHOTOGRAPH FROM THE LIBRARY OF CONGRESS HAS BEEN PAINTED WITH AN AMERICAN FLAG OF THAT TIME AND A PATRIOTIC MESSAGE.

Little more than twenty-seven years to the day later, on November 24, 1924, that same dogged determination would bring Edwin Hubble to the attention of the world as the man who would forever change humankind's concept of the universe and our place in it.

HUBBLE WAS BARELY FOURTEEN YEARS OLD WHEN ORVILLE AND WILBUR WRIGHT MADE THE FIRST SUCCESSFUL POWERED AIRPLANE FLIGHT WITH A HUMAN ON BOARD AT KITTY HAWK ON NORTH CAROLINA'S OUTER BANKS. MANY SCIENTISTS REGARD HUBBLE'S WORK TO BE AS GREAT A BREAK-THROUGH IN ASTRONOMY AS THE WRIGHT BROTHERS' INVENTION WAS IN TECHNOLOGY.

FAMILY LIFE

The third of eight children of John and Virginia Lee James Hubble, Edwin was born in a time of great progress. The year before young Edwin first gazed through a telescope, Henry Ford produced his first automobile in Detroit, Michigan. And less than a month after Edwin's fourteenth birthday, the Wright brothers successfully flew the first powered airplane at Kitty Hawk, North Carolina.

Though John Hubble had studied law, he joined the family's insurance business. This forced his growing family to move to Springfield, Missouri, where the headquarters of the insurance company he worked for was located. They then moved to the suburbs of Chicago, Illinois, first in Evanston and finally to Wheaton.

The Hubbles were a close-knit and well-to-do family, watched over by a stern father and a tolerant mother. Both parents taught their children a strong sense of family and responsibility. Edwin was an avid reader of adventure novels, including the fantastic tales of pioneer science fiction writers Jules Verne and H. Rider Haggard. These combined with his interest in astronomy, launched by his grandfather. At age twelve, he wrote his grandfather a letter that predicted the possibility of life on Mars. He graduated from high school in 1906 and was awarded a scholarship to the University of Chicago for his academic achievements.

LEARNING FROM THE BEST

Edwin Hubble came to the University of Chicago at a time when it was home to a number of eminent astronomers and physicists. In addition, the university housed the Yerkes Observatory. The observatory then, as now, contained the largest refractor telescope in the world, the 40-inch (102-centimeter) telescope created by the pioneer astrophysicist, George Ellery Hale

(1868–1938), in 1897. A refractor telescope uses a giant lens to gather light.

Majoring in mathematics and astronomy, Hubble had access to scholars like Professor Hale and to that magnificent telescope. While he had been free to observe whatever he wished as an eight-year-old through his grandfather's small telescope, observing time at Yerkes was precious. The giant refractor was booked for specific projects, mostly solar observations, which was Hale's area of specialization. Hubble worked on one of Hale's projects, the study and photographing of the sun during its active sunspot cycles.

Edwin Hubble graduated from the University of Chicago and was awarded a Rhodes scholarship for postgraduate study at a university in England. The Rhodes is given to students with superior academic records who also excel in sports and display good character traits.

Concerned that he might not be able to make an adequate living in mathematics and astronomy, Hubble chose not to pursue his scientific studies. Instead, he enrolled in Oxford University's Queen's College to study law. The young American made the most of his three years at Oxford, spending his summers traveling through Germany, France, and Switzerland.

DISCOVERING NEBULAE

At the end of his three years abroad, Hubble returned home with a bachelor's degree. He taught school, translated documents from German to English, and even worked with a group of surveyors mapping a railroad line through the northern Wisconsin wilderness.

By the spring of 1914, Hubble had apparently reached a decision about what he wanted to do with his life. He wrote to Forest Ray Moulton, his old teacher at the University of Chicago, to apply as a graduate student. Edwin R. Frost, the director of Yerkes

Observatory, accepted Hubble and arranged for the returning student to receive a scholarship. He also invited Hubble to accompany him to a meeting of the American Astronomical Society at Northwestern University in August of 1914.

It was at the meeting—where Hubble was elected a member of the prestigious organization—that he first became interested in the mysterious objects known as nebulae (from the Latin word *nebula*, or "cloud"). There were two types of nebulae recognized during this period. The first was a cloudy formation of dust and gas. The second was a faint, fuzzy object that was spiral in shape. This was known as a spiral nebula.

Spiral nebulae are flattened, rotating disks of groups of young stars, with a central bulge and a surrounding halo of older stars. They also contain dense groups of old stars called globular clusters, which were Hubble's own area of specialty. The nature of spiral nebulae was uncertain at the time, though. Astronomers knew that the Milky Way looked the way it did because it was made up of many stars at a great distance from the solar system. Some astronomers thought spiral nebulae were made of similar collections of bright stars even farther away than the Milky Way. Other astronomers thought they were closer collections but composed of faint stars or gas.

Nebulae in general appeared to observers on Earth as though they were not moving. But a paper delivered by American astronomer Dr. Vesto M. Slipher (1875–1969)

AFTER RETURNING FROM ENGLAND AND WORKING FOR A SHORT TIME, HUBBLE DECIDED TO RETURN TO THE UNIVERSITY OF CHICAGO FOR POSTGRADUATE STUDY IN ASTRONOMY. HE SOON BECAME FASCINATED WITH NEBULAE, SUCH AS THE FAMOUS WHIRLPOOL (ALSO KNOWN AS M51, OR THE 51ST OBJECT IN A 1771 CATALOG OF NEBULAE BY CHARLES MESSIER), SHOWN HERE IN AN IMAGE PRODUCED BY THE HUBBLE SPACE TELESCOPE.

presented photographic evidence that proved otherwise. The evidence was in the colors of the light when passed through a spectroscope. Compared to ordinary starlight, the spectrum of thirteen nebulae was shifted toward the red by an astonishingly large amount.

Slipher concluded that the large redshift is evidence that those nebulae are receding, or moving away from Earth, at incredibly high speeds through space. Though Slipher's calculations and radical conclusion were dismissed by many of his fellow astronomers as sloppy research, Hubble wasn't so sure. He was intrigued by the scientific puzzle over what it meant if the nebulae were in fact receding. He decided to investigate for himself.

SLIPHER AND THE SPECTRUM OF STARLIGHT

Since the mid-nineteenth century, astronomers have been studying stars by spreading out their light into a spectrum. They first used prisms to produce a band of colors from red to violet, but now they use other devices that allow them to examine the light from stars and planets in a range that can go deep into the infrared or the far ultraviolet. The spectrum is mainly a continuous band of changing color, but it is crossed by a series of dark, narrow lines produced when gases in the outer regions of stars absorb some light. The positions of those lines tell scientists what gases are absorbing the light.

The spectra of the nebulae Slipher was studying showed a series of lines that were spaced exactly like those produced by hydrogen, but were shifted toward the red end of the spectrum. The spectrum of some individual stars showed small redshifts, and astronomers agreed that meant they were moving away from the solar system. But the spectra Slipher observed for spiral nebulae were redshifted by a much larger amount. That suggested that they were moving away at speeds that were far beyond what anyone had ever imagined was possible.

HUBBLE'S DOCTORAL RESEARCH

Slipher's results gave Hubble a perfect starting point for his own research. At the Yerkes Observatory's smaller 24-inch (61-cm) telescope, Hubble set out to determine the spectra of other distant spiral nebulae. By comparing his photographic plates against those made of the same section of the sky a decade earlier, he discovered a dozen spiral nebulae whose light was also redshifted. These were the faintest objects in which any motion had been found. But recalling the hostile reception to Slipher's controversial findings, he was hesitant to go public with his conclusions until he had more evidence.

The study of spiral nebulae was still new, and their origin and composition were unknown. The explanation of the mystery of their movement depended on how far from Earth they were located. If, as was believed at the time, the entire universe was only a few thousand light-years across, their makeup was most likely collections of glowing interstellar dust and gas, lit from behind by even more distant stars. But if, as Hubble supposed, the universe was far larger than believed, these cloudy smudges against the blackness of space might just be star systems at distances of millions of light years.

WITHIN A FEW YEARS OF COMPLETING HIS DOCTORAL RESEARCH, EDWIN HUBBLE, SHOWN HERE AS A YOUNG MAN, WOULD REVOLUTIONIZE COSMOLOGY, THE STUDY OF THE UNIVERSE ITSELF. HE ESTABLISHED THAT MOST NEBULAE ARE GALAXIES— SYSTEMS OF BILLIONS OF STARS—IN AN EXPANDING UNIVERSE FAR LARGER THAN ASTRONOMERS HAD PREVIOUSLY THOUGHT IT TO BE.

Hubble finished his doctoral dissertation, "Photographic Investigations of Faint Nebulae," in 1917. He was a newcomer to the study of nebulae, which was itself a new field of study. Although nearly two thousand nebulae had so far been discovered, they could not yet be positively identified as being made of stars.

Still, Hubble's research was an important step on the road to identifying what spiral nebulae were. But he did not suspect that the next steps would lead to a new view of the nature of the universe itself.

CHAPTER TWO

FROM ASTRONOMY TO COSMOLOGY

From the first time Edwin Hubble looked through his grandfather's telescope, he was already on his way to a life in the science of astronomy. As he grew and learned more about the objects in the night sky, he also realized that many discoveries lay ahead. When he returned to the University of Chicago as a graduate student, he expected to contribute to the science of astronomy by observing something in the universe that no one before him had ever seen.

But what new question about the solar system or the stars could he try to answer? When he heard about Slipher's work with spiral nebulae, he realized that it led to more questions than it answered. That would be an area of astronomy where he could make a small contribution. He never expected his findings to transform the way people looked at the universe as a whole.

CHANGING VIEWS OF THE UNIVERSE

Cosmology, the study of the universe as a whole, can be traced back to ancient Greek philosophers from the fourth century BCE. They studied the movements of the planets and other celestial bodies across the night sky and developed a cosmological model to interpret what they saw.

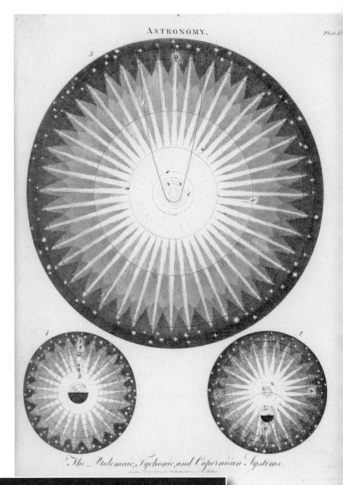

Not surprisingly, the Greeks placed the Earth as an unmoving object at the center of the universe, around which all else revolved. We call that a geocentric (or Earth-centered) cosmological theory. Because everything seemed to follow a predictable path, and since the heavens seemed to be an example

SHOWN HERE ARE THREE DRAWINGS THAT ILLUSTRATE HOW SCIENTIFIC UNDERSTANDING OF THE UNIVERSE CHANGED OVER HISTORY. AT THE LOWER LEFT IS THE EARTH-CENTERED SYSTEM DEVISED BY THE SECOND-CENTURY EGYPTIAN-BORN GREEK ASTRONOMER PTOLEMY. THAT MODEL OF THE UNIVERSE DOMINATED SCIENTIFIC THOUGHT UNTIL NICOLAUS COPERNICUS DESCRIBED A SUN-CENTERED SYSTEM IN THE 16TH CENTURY (TOP). NOT WANTING TO GIVE UP THE CENTRAL POSITION OF EARTH BUT RECOGNIZING THE VALUE OF THE COPERNICAN MODEL, TYCHO BRAHE PROPOSED THAT THE PLANETS ORBITED THE SUN WHILE THE SUN ORBITED EARTH.

of perfection, their geocentric universe behaved like a well-designed but complex machine. Everything in that machine had to move in perfect circles and at constant speed.

With such a machine, the most difficult motions to understand were the planets, which occasionally reversed their movement from east to west across the zodiac. The more they observed the movements of the planets, the more complex the machinery had to be. By the second century CE, the Egyptian-Greek philosopher and mathematician Ptolemy had come up with a model that seemed to account for the motions of the sun, moon, stars, and planets. This came to be known as the Ptolemaic system.

We now know that this apparent reversal of the planets is because Earth is a planet, too. It, like the other planets, revolves around the sun. The farther away a planet is from the sun, the slower it moves in its orbit. From our perspective on Earth, we usually see a planet moving from east to west across the zodiac. But occasionally, because of the combination of our motion and the planet's motion, we see the planet moving from west to east.

So the geocentric model is simply wrong, but Ptolemy didn't know that. Ptolemy described his system in an enormous volume entitled the *Almagest*. In that book, he added three mathematical elements that brought the planets' motions in line with the idea that heavenly objects must move in perfect circles at constant speeds. Instead of having the Earth at the exact center of the planet's circular path, he added a point called the equant.

The sun traveled in a circle around Earth, but its speed on that circle was not constant. Instead, the angle it made with the equant changed at a constant

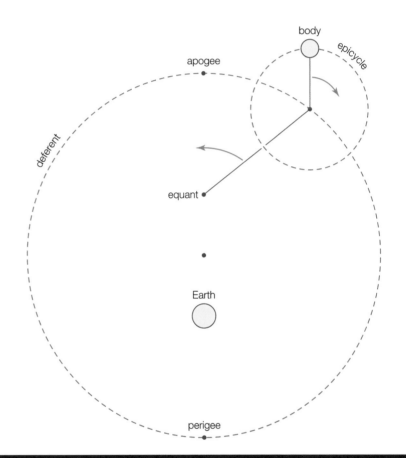

IN THE *ALMAGEST*, PTOLEMY DESCRIBED THE MOTION OF THE SUN, THE MOON, OR A PLANET AS A COMBINATION OF TWO CIRCULAR MOTIONS AT CONSTANT RATES. THE BODY'S MAIN MOTION WAS AROUND A LARGE CIRCLE CALLED THE DEFERENT, WHICH WAS CENTERED ON A POINT HALFWAY BETWEEN EARTH AND ANOTHER POINT CALLED THE EQUANT. FOR EACH BODY, A SMALLER CIRCLE CALLED THE EPICYCLE WAS CENTERED ON A POINT THAT TRAVELED AROUND THE DEFERENT. THE SUN'S SPEED AROUND THE DEFERENT WAS NOT CONSTANT. INSTEAD, ITS SPEED VARIED SO THAT THE ANGLE IT MADE WITH THE EQUANT CHANGED AT A CONSTANT RATE.

rate. The midpoint of the line segment between Earth and the equant was the center of a circle called the deferent, or the main circular path, for each planet. The equant and deferent were still not enough to solve the mismatch between his math and the actual motion, so for each planet, he added a smaller circle, called an epicycle, going around a point on the larger circle. That seemed to solve the problem.

Over the centuries, the Ptolemaic system needed to be adjusted with epicycles being added to epicycles. But it was not seriously challenged until the Polish astronomer Nicolaus Copernicus (1473–1543) introduced a heliocentric (or sun-centered) model of the solar system. By moving the Earth into an orbit around the sun and having it rotate on its axis once a day, the Copernican model eliminated the deferent, equant, and some epicycles. But Copernicus still required perfect circular motion at constant speed, so most of the epicycles remained.

Like many other astronomers of the time, however, the Danish astronomer Tycho Brahe (1546–1601) rejected the part of Copernicus's theory that placed the Earth in motion. Brahe developed his own model of the universe in which the planets orbited the sun, while the sun orbited Earth. He thought that if the Earth were moving around the sun, then the stars in the sky would appear to be in different positions as the Earth made its way around its orbit. This apparent change in the position of an object when viewed against a background from different vantage points is known as parallax. To Brahe, the stars appeared to have fixed positions in the sky, but in fact, there is parallax. Brahe didn't see it because it was too small for his instruments to detect, even though they were the best in the world at that time.

COSMIC EVIDENCE, COSMIC CHANGES

It was the Italian scientist Galileo Galilei (1564–1642) who offered the most convincing evidence of the heliocentric model. The first to turn a telescope toward the sky, Galileo discovered mountains on the moon, showing that heavenly bodies are not perfect. He observed that Venus went through phases like the moon, confirming that it orbits closer to the sun than Earth does. And he discovered four moons orbiting the planet Jupiter. If a moon could orbit a planet, he reasoned, then a planet could orbit the sun. His 1632 work, *Dialogue Concerning the Two Chief World Systems, Ptolemaic and Copernican*, proved to be a turning point in astronomical thought.

While Galileo was observing with the telescope, the German astronomer Johannes Kepler (1571–1630) was observing the planets in the observatory founded by Brahe and developing mathematical formulas that described their orbits. Those became known as his three laws, and they applied to Earth's orbit as well as

HOW TO DRAW AN ELLIPSE

Not just any oval will do as an ellipse. If you choose any two points on an ellipse, such as the ones marked P and Q on the diagram, the sum of the distances from P to A and P to B must be equal to the sum of the distances from Q to A and Q to B.

It is easy to draw an ellipse on a piece of cardboard by sticking in two thumbtacks an inch or two apart near the center of the cardboard. Their positions correspond to points A and B, which will be the two foci of the ellipse. Then make a loop of string around both thumbtacks. The loop should be a few inches longer than the distance between A and B when it is stretched to its limit. But it should be short enough that when stretched in any direction, it stays on the cardboard. Now stretch the loop with a pencil, and keeping it tight, draw an oval. That oval is an ellipse.

If the pencil point represents a planet, then one of the thumbtacks is the sun. The farther apart the two foci are compared to the length of the string, the more elongated is the ellipse. If the two thumbtacks are so close together that they overlap, the ellipse becomes a circle.

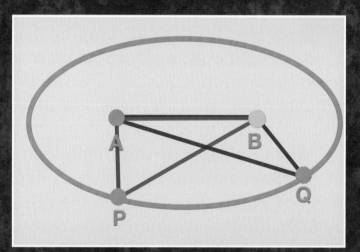

the orbits of the other five known planets. Thus they strengthened the heliocentric model.

The orbit of Mars was particularly revealing. By studying it, he concluded that the planets travel around the sun in elliptical paths, not in perfect circles. By replacing Copernicus's circular orbits with ellipses, Kepler was able to do away with epicycles. That is his first law. An ellipse is a particular kind of oval with two points inside it called the foci (plural of focus). A circle is an ellipse for which the two foci overlap at a single point. For the planets' elliptical orbits, the sun is at one focus. This means that during its orbital cycle, a planet will sometimes move closer to the sun and sometimes move farther away.

Kepler's other two laws gave mathematical formulas for the orbits, but they didn't explain the cause of

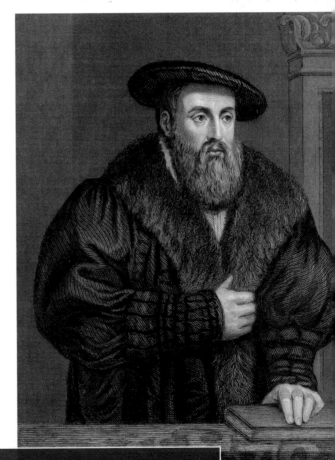

BY STUDYING THE OBSERVATIONS OF TYCHO BRAHE AND ADDING HIS OWN DATA, JOHANNES KEPLER DISCOVERED THAT THE ORBIT OF MARS WAS AN ELLIPSE. HE THEN REALIZED THAT ALL THE PLANETS ALSO FOLLOWED ELLIPTICAL PATHS AROUND THE SUN, A FACT THAT PEOPLE NOW REFER TO AS KEPLER'S FIRST LAW. HE ALSO DEVELOPED TWO OTHER MATHEMATICAL LAWS DESCRIBING PLANETARY MOTION.

those formulas. That explanation came in 1687, when the English mathematician and physicist Isaac Newton (1642–1727) published his *Philosophiae Naturalis Principia Mathematica (Mathematical Principles of Natural Philosophy)*, which included his theory of gravity and gave a mathematical explanation for Kepler's laws.

Another important discovery came in 1838 when

the German astronomer and mathematician Friedrich Wilhelm Bessel (1784–1846) measured the parallax of the star 61 Cygni from the Earth and determined its distance to be approximately 10.3 light-years or about 60.5 trillion miles from Earth— nearly 650,000 times as far as the Earth's 93 million-mile (150 million-kilometer) distance from the sun.

IN 1755, GERMAN PHILOSOPHER IMMANUEL KANT, SHOWN HERE IN A 1791 PAINTING BY GOTTLIEB DOEBLER, PROPOSED THAT THE MILKY WAY WAS A BAND OF DISTANT STARS AT THE EDGE OF OUR UNIVERSE. HE ALSO SUGGESTED THAT THERE MIGHT BE OTHER "ISLAND UNIVERSES" TOO FAR AWAY TO BE SEEN. FEW PEOPLE ACCEPTED THAT IDEA UNTIL HUBBLE'S DISCOVERY OF GALAXIES, WHICH WERE EXACTLY LIKE THE ISLAND UNIVERSES KANT HAD ENVISIONED.

Today's best measurements put its distance at 11.4 light-years. By then astronomers realized that the sun was one of many stars in the cosmos. It was certainly the center of the solar system, but there was no longer any reason to say that it was in the center of the whole universe.

Astronomers were not the only ones who were proposing new ideas about the cosmos. In 1755, German philosopher Immanuel Kant (1724–1804) proposed that the Milky Way was made up of many distant stars and was the edge of our universe. But he proposed that our universe might actually be one of a very large number of "island universes," each very much like our own but too far away and too dim to be seen from the solar system.

Kant never used the word "galaxy," and most people didn't accept his idea of island universes without evidence. But nearly two centuries later Hubble found that evidence. His observations of spiral nebulae would reveal that they were exactly the kind of island universes that Kant had envisioned. And that was only part of the story. The distance of those island universes revealed a much larger universe than anyone had imagined. And even more astonishing was their motion, which suggested that the universe was expanding like a balloon.

CHAPTER THREE

GALAXIES

In April 1917, Hubble completed his doctoral thesis. His research was so outstanding that it earned him an invitation from his old University of Chicago professor, George Ellery Hale, to join the staff at the newly completed Mount Wilson Observatory of the California Institute of Technology (Caltech) in Pasadena.

Hale's offer was precisely the kind of job Hubble was looking for. But history intervened. Europe had been at war since 1914, but the United States had avoided taking sides. Finally, on April 2, 1917, United States president Woodrow Wilson asked Congress to declare war on Germany. When Congress passed a declaration of war, the European conflict became a world war, which is now known as World War I.

The day after finishing his doctoral thesis, Edwin Hubble joined the United States Army. Hubble sent Hale his reluctant regrets and reported instead to officer's training camp at Fort Sheridan, Illinois. By December of 1917, he had achieved the rank of major. He shipped out to Europe in September 1918. Though willing to do his part in combat, he had arrived too late. The war was nearly over, and on November 11, it ended. Nine months later he was released from the military. He headed directly for Pasadena where Professor Hale still had an opening at the Mount Wilson Observatory for the promising new astronomer.

WHEN HUBBLE WAS AN UNDERGRADUATE STUDENT AT THE UNIVERSITY OF CHICAGO, HE WORKED ON ONE OF PROFESSOR GEORGE ELLERY HALE'S PROJECTS OBSERVING SUNSPOTS, AS HALE IS DOING IN THIS 1907 PHOTOGRAPH AT THE MOUNT WILSON OBSERVATORY IN CALIFORNIA. AFTER COMPLETING HIS PH.D. DEGREE IN 1917, HUBBLE APPLIED FOR AND WAS OFFERED A JOB WITH HALE AT MOUNT WILSON. WORLD WAR I INTERVENED, AND HUBBLE ENLISTED IN THE U.S. ARMY INSTEAD. HALE HELD THE JOB OPEN UNTIL HUBBLE RETURNED IN 1919.

THE MYSTERY OF SPIRAL NEBULAE

When Edwin Hubble and George Hale had last worked together, Hale had mainly been interested in the study of the sun. Since then, however, he had become in-

trigued by spiral nebulae, in large part because of Slipher's results and his own thesis research.

At the Mount Wilson Observatory, Hubble sought to discover more spiral nebulae and measure their distances from Earth. Were they closer or farther away than the stars of the Milky Way, which are about one hundred thousand light-years away? Because the ones he

HUBBLE ARRIVED AT MOUNT WILSON NOT LONG AFTER HALE'S BRAINCHILD, THE HOOKER TELESCOPE WITH A 100-INCH (254-CM) MIRROR, WAS COMPLETED. AT THAT TIME, IT WAS THE LARGEST TELESCOPE OF ITS KIND, AND HUBBLE USED IT TO STUDY THE SKY FOR DISTANT GALAXIES. HIS DISCOVERY OF CEPHEID VARIABLE STARS IN OTHER GALAXIES GAVE HIM A WAY TO MEASURE THEIR DISTANCES, AND MEASURING THE "RED SHIFT" IN THEIR SPECTRA ENABLED HIM TO DETERMINE HOW FAST THEY WERE MOVING AWAY FROM THE SOLAR SYSTEM.

had already studied seemed to be moving away at such high speeds, he believed they could be millions of light-years farther. That would mean the universe was much larger than astronomers thought. But if the nebulae were that far from the solar system, their parallax would be too small to give a good measurement. Fortunately, he had another technique in mind.

He began his studies by photographing a large area of the night sky as far from Earth as the giant Hooker Telescope could see. Night after night, he sat at the telescope exposing photographic plates until he knew the sky and its countless stars as intimately as another man might know the layout of his own home.

Measuring the cosmic distances between stars was then, as today, no simple task. In 1912, Henrietta Swan Leavitt (1868–1921), an astronomer at the Harvard College Observatory, was assigned to catalog a certain class of stars called Cepheid variables, named after the constellation Cepheus in which the first one was discovered. Their brightness changed from bright to dim and back, pulsating at a steady rate. Leavitt discovered a mathematical relationship between cycle time and average luminosity, or the average amount of light that a Cepheid gave off.

Using Leavitt's formula and measuring a Cepheid's cycle time, an astronomer would know exactly how brightly it is shining. And by measuring its apparent luminosity, or how bright it seems to be, an

CEPHEIDS AS "STANDARD CANDLES"

When cataloging data from Cepheids in the Magellanic clouds, which were too far away for their distance to be measured by parallax, Henrietta Leavitt noticed something unusual. The brighter stars had longer periods of pulsation than the dimmer ones. Since they were all at about the same distance, that meant that a Cepheid's actual brightness and its period of pulsation are related in a predictable way.

From the distance and measured brightness of nearby Cepheids, whose distances were accurately known, Leavitt could compute the actual brightness and produce a mathematical relationship between that and the pulsation rate. That relationship allowed her to use Cepheid variables as "standard candles" (lights whose brightness is known) and to compute the distance to the Magellanic clouds.

In the same way, astronomers can calculate the distance to any Cepheid variable in any galaxy merely by measuring its pulsation rate.

ALTHOUGH HUBBLE DID NOT KNOW IT AT THE TIME, EVERY GALAXY HAS A SUPERMASSIVE BLACK HOLE AT ITS CENTER. A BLACK HOLE HAS SO MUCH MASS THAT NOT EVEN LIGHT CAN ESCAPE FROM ITS GRAVITY BUT IT CAN BE DETECTED BY THE GLOW OF HOT GASES THAT ARE FALLING INTO IT. THIS HUBBLE SPACE TELESCOPE IMAGE SHOWS THE GLOW AROUND THE BLACK HOLE, WITH A MASS EQUAL TO THAT OF 100 MILLION SUNS, IN THE NEIGHBORING ANDROMEDA GALAXY.

M31 Nucleus

Hubble Space Telescope • ACS/HRC

HST ACS/HRC

WIYN/KPNO 0.9m Mosaic I

NASA, ESA, and T. Lauer (NOAO)

STScI-PRC12-04a

astronomer can then determine how far away it is. Specifically, the apparent luminosity decreases in proportion to the square of the distance between the star and the observer. So, for objects with the same brightness, an object that appears one ten-thousandth as bright as another would have to be one hundred times farther away. This is how the distances of Cepheids were calculated.

By the time Hubble was making his observations, another Mount Wilson astronomer, Harlow Shapley (1885–1972), had already measured the size of the Milky Way. Like Hubble, Shapley used Cepheids to make his measurements of globular clusters in the Milky Way. From this, he calculated it to be some one hundred thousand light-years away.

Still, Shapley was one of the most vocal critics of the so-called island universe theory put forth by Kant and others since the nineteenth century. The nebulae that so intrigued Hubble, Shapley insisted, were nothing more than relatively nearby clouds of glowing gas. But by October of 1923, Hubble had found the evidence that would convince the rest of the scientific community.

ANDROMEDA TELLS THE TALE

Hubble's evidence was a Cepheid variable that he discovered in the Andromeda nebula, which he

had been observing through the Mount Wilson telescope. A single photographic plate of Andromeda (of-
ficially classified as M31) showed the Cepheid. This
was labeled in Hubble's own hand as "VAR!" and was
the linchpin of Hubble's remarkable discovery. It appeared to be much fainter than closer Cepheids with
the same cycle, so he knew it was much farther away.

Hubble's calculations were startling, showing that
the faint patch of light was actually about 2.5 million light-years from Earth, or about 600,000 times
more distant than the nearest stars and 25 times as
far away as the stars of the Milky Way. This was clear
evidence supporting the island universe theory. These
island universes came to be called galaxies, after the
Greek word for milk. And the galaxy that contains the
solar system came to be known as the Milky Way galaxy after the band of stars that we see that marks its
farthest edge.

So Hubble discovered that the Milky Way galaxy,
as large as it may have seemed, is not the whole universe. Like other galaxies, it is a cluster of gas, dust,
and billions of stars that are held together by gravitational attraction. We now know that it was one of
tens or hundreds of billions of similar galaxies spread
across an unimaginably huge universe. Andromeda,
though 2.5 million light-years away is actually our
nearest neighbor. Thanks to Edwin Hubble's discovery,
Kant's island universe idea was shown to be correct.

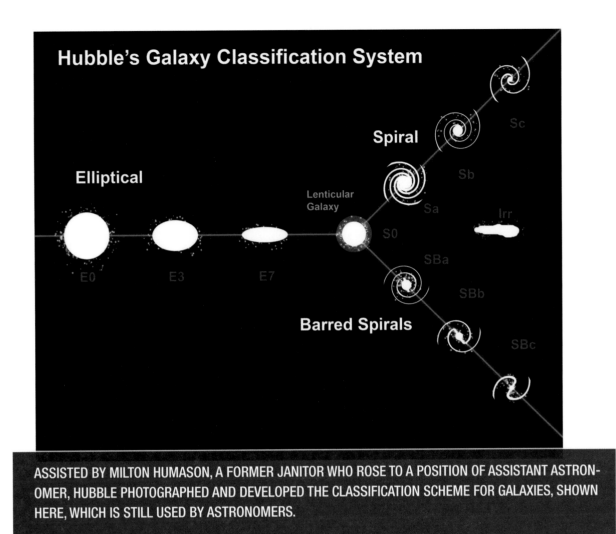

Hubble's Galaxy Classification System

ASSISTED BY MILTON HUMASON, A FORMER JANITOR WHO ROSE TO A POSITION OF ASSISTANT ASTRONOMER, HUBBLE PHOTOGRAPHED AND DEVELOPED THE CLASSIFICATION SCHEME FOR GALAXIES, SHOWN HERE, WHICH IS STILL USED BY ASTRONOMERS.

On November 23, 1924, shortly after Hubble returned from an extended honeymoon in Europe, a headline in the *New York Times* read "Finds Spiral Nebulae are Stellar Systems. Doctor Hubbell [sic] Confirms View they are 'Island Universes.'" The article reported Hubble's findings and made him an overnight celebrity. But the newly prominent astronomer had already set his sights on a new puzzle.

CLASSIFYING GALAXIES

Hubble decided that the next step in his study of the universe was to develop a classification system for the newly discovered galaxies. He was assisted by Milton Humason (1891–1972), a man with an elementary school education who rose from janitor at the Mount Wilson Observatory to a position as assistant astronomer. He was now one of the leading experts in the field, eventually becoming an astronomer at the Mount Wilson and Palomar Observatories.

Together, they set out to photograph as many nebulae as they could, classifying them according to shape: elliptical, spiral, barred spiral, and, for those galaxies that conformed to no other categories, irregular. With these basic shapes he introduced a system of classification that scientists use to this very day. Hubble presented their system, complete with photographic plates, in a paper in a 1926 issue of the *Astrophysical Journal*.

THE EXPANDING UNIVERSE

Light from a star could be analyzed by looking at it through a device called a spectroscope. During Hubble's time, spectroscopes (or spectrometers) used prisms, or pieces of triangular-shaped translucent glass or crystal, to separate light into the colors of the visible spectrum: red, orange, yellow, green, blue, indigo, and violet. The same principle of a spectrum is at work when sunlight passes through raindrops in the atmosphere, producing a rainbow.

Modern spectroscopes use devices called diffraction gratings to spread out the light more broadly for more precise measurements. They also make it possible to study light beyond the visible range, either in the ultraviolet or the infrared portions of the spectrum.

By viewing the light from an object through a spectrometer, scientists can measure its temperature and can often tell what an object is made of. The bands of colors, or spectral lines, represent different elements, ions, and compounds. Thus, an observer on Earth can tell the chemical makeup of a star even hundreds of millions of light-years away. The presence of a particular chemical shows up as a set of narrow dark lines across the bright spectrum. These occur because the star puts out light at all colors or wavelengths, but each element, compound, or ion in the star's outer regions absorbs its own particular set of wavelengths, which makes the light dimmer at those wavelengths.

For stars within the Milky Way galaxy, the spectral lines of their elements (such as helium, hydrogen, calcium, and titanium, all of which are present in our sun) appear at almost exactly the same position of the lines from the spectrum of the sun. The pattern of lines may be shifted a slight amount toward the blue or red end of the spectrum, but it takes a very accurate spectrometer to detect that. For all but a few galaxies, however,

Hubble discovered that the light is redshifted by a large amount. Andromeda is an exception; its light is shifted toward the blue.

The reason for the shift is a phenomenon known as the Doppler effect, which is a change in the wavelength and frequency of a wave caused by the motion of its source or the receiver. For instance, we experience the Doppler effect in the case of an approaching fire truck siren. The sound it makes as it approaches gets higher in pitch, changing once it passes us to a lower pitch. This is because when the truck approaches us, the sound waves from the siren get pushed together, increasing the frequency, or the number of wave crests that pass within a certain time. A higher frequency corresponds to a higher pitch. When the truck moves away from us, the wavelengths become longer and the frequency lowers, thus lowering the pitch.

THE DISCOVERY OF HELIUM

Helium is a well-known element that gets its name from *helios*, the Greek word for "sun." That is because before it was discovered on Earth, it was discovered in 1868 as a set of dark lines in the light of the solar spectrum. It was hard to detect on Earth because it does not react with other elements. It was finally spotted in 1895 by studying the spectrum of a gas coming out of uranium ore.

With light, higher frequency corresponds to shifting spectral lines toward the shorter wavelength or blue end of the spectrum. When the source of light and the receiver are moving apart, the frequency decreases and the wavelength increases, making the color of the light shift toward the red.

For all galaxies, with the exception of our closest neighbors like Andromeda, which is moving toward the Milky Way galaxy, Hubble observed a substantial redshift. He also measured the galaxies' distances using Cepheid variables and discovered that the farther away the galaxy was, the greater its redshift. He used the redshift and the equations of the Doppler effect to calculate how fast those galaxies were moving away from Earth.

With these two pieces of information, he found a simple proportion between the distance of the galaxies and how fast they were moving away (or receding) from us. In other words, the ratio of a galaxy's speed of recession (v) to its distance from the solar system (r) has the same value, H_0, which scientists now call the Hubble constant. Stated as an equation, that is "$H_0 = v/r$ or $v = H_0 r$." That means that a galaxy that is one hundred million light-years away from Earth recedes twice as fast as a galaxy that is fifty million light-years away. To determine the speed, simply multiply the distance by the Hubble constant. Some of the most distant objects Hubble was able to observe were receding at speeds of up to 90 percent of the speed of light, which meant they were billions of light years away. Hubble published this discovery in the *Proceedings of the National Academy of Sciences* as "A Relation Between Distance And Radial Velocity Among Extra-Galactic Nebulae."

That finding was revolutionary. Instead of being uniform and steady, as most theories of cosmology expected at the time, the universe was expanding like a balloon with clusters of galaxies all spreading apart from one another. Hubble's law soon became the foundation of a new theory of the origin of the universe, which we now know as the big bang theory.

THE EXPANDING UNIVERSE AND THE THEORY OF RELATIVITY

When German born physicist Albert Einstein (1879–1955) heard about Hubble's results, he immediately began to reconsider one key part of the theory that had gained him international acclaim, the theory of relativity. That theory took several years to develop fully, but it began with Einstein's first publication in 1905 on the topic of the special theory of relativity.

The word "special" refers to the fact that it deals with the motion of bodies at a constant speed relative to one

ALBERT EINSTEIN, SEEN HERE ON THE LEFT VISITING THE MOUNT WILSON OBSERVATORY, BELIEVED THAT THE UNIVERSE MUST BE IN A STEADY STATE. SO HE WAS TROUBLED THAT HE HAD TO ADD A "COSMOLOGICAL CONSTANT" TO HIS GENERAL THEORY OF RELATIVITY TO PREVENT IT FROM PREDICTING A UNIVERSE THAT WAS EITHER EXPANDING OR CONTRACTING. HUBBLE'S DISCOVERY THAT THE UNIVERSE WAS EXPANDING ALLOWED EINSTEIN TO REMOVE THE CONSTANT, WHICH HE THEN CALLED HIS GREATEST BLUNDER.

another. It redefined the way space and time are measured, especially when the relative speed of the objects involved is approaching the speed of light in a vacuum (approximately 186,000 miles per second or just under 300,000 kilometers per second). One of Einstein's key results is that nothing can travel faster than the speed of light. Another key result is that space and time are interrelated and should be viewed together as space-time.

It took Einstein an additional ten years to develop the general theory of relativity, which he published in 1915. It deals with bodies that are changing their relative velocity. One of the most remarkable predictions of the general theory was that mass causes a warping of space-time just as a bowling ball warps the surface of a mattress full of springs. If you put some smaller balls on that same mattress, they will roll toward the bowling ball as if it attracted them by gravity.

The equations of general relativity are complex, but they reveal that gravitational attraction is the result of the warping of space-time by a massive body. That warping causes planets to move in elliptical orbits. More surprisingly, the general theory also predicts that the warping of space-time also causes light not to follow a straight line when it passes by a heavy object like the sun.

That prediction could not be verified easily since any light that passes close to the sun would be lost in the sun's glare—except during a solar eclipse. Then we can see stars during the day that are normally visible at night during the opposite season (six months earlier or later). If Einstein's prediction was correct, the starlight would bend toward the sun, which means we would see the stars shifted slightly farther away from the sun than expected.

In 1919, two teams of scientists observed a solar eclipse and carefully measured the position of the stars closest to the sun in the sky. They found their positions shifted by the amount that Einstein had predicted. That astonishing result made headlines around the world, and Einstein became a celebrity. Still, he was troubled by one aspect of his general theory. In order to have a uniform, steady universe, he needed to include a factor that he called the cosmological constant. Otherwise, the theory predicted that space-time was either steadily expanding or contracting.

When Hubble's work showed an expanding universe, Einstein was delighted. He could drop the cosmological constant from his theory, and he went to his grave believing that the constant was the "greatest blunder" he ever made. However, his greatest mistake may have actually been calling the constant a blunder in the first place.

CHAPTER FOUR

LOOKING BACKWARD IN TIME

I f we live in an expanding universe, as Hubble's results suggest, what did the universe look like in the past? To answer that question, you need to reverse the motion as if you are viewing a movie in reverse. In the backward-running movie, an expanding universe becomes a contracting universe. Eventually it reaches some time in the distant past, which we can call time zero, when everything was together in a single point.

That means that instead of being uniform and unchanging for all time, the universe had a definite beginning. At time zero, space-time and all the matter in the universe came into being in a great explosion and began expanding. We now call that explosion "the big bang." From everything we now know about matter and energy, the backward-running movie makes sense at least until the very earliest fraction of a fraction of a microsecond. And physicists are still trying to understand what happened in that near-instant of time.

FRIEDMANN, LEMAÎTRE, AND THE EXPANDING UNIVERSE

After Einstein proposed his general theory of relativity, other physicists and mathematicians struggled to understand what it might be telling us about the universe. In particular, in 1922 Russian physicist and mathematician Alexander Friedmann (1888–1925), used it to analyze a universe in which objects are evenly distributed everywhere. On the cosmic scale, this means that the observation of distant galaxies in every direction shows there to be a more or less equal

ALEXANDER FRIEDMANN WAS A RUSSIAN MATHEMATICIAN WHO APPLIED EINSTEIN'S GENERAL THEORY OF RELATIVITY TO COSMOLOGY AND CONCLUDED THAT THE UNIVERSE MUST BE EXPANDING. HE DIED OF TYPHOID FEVER AT AGE THIRTY-SEVEN IN 1925, FOUR YEARS BEFORE HUBBLE'S DISCOVERY SHOWED THAT HIS CONCLUSION WAS CORRECT.

number of galaxies no matter where we look. And that would be the same for all other observers, no matter where in the universe they are.

To all observers, this would give the impression that they are at the center of the universe. But in fact, Einstein's special theory of relativity shows that there is no center since all motion is relative. No matter where our location is anywhere in the universe, the amount of matter we see—that is, the number of visible stars and galaxies—should be more or less the same.

Friedmann's math led to some surprising conclusions, including that even with the cosmological constant, the universe could not be unchanging unless it had no mass in it. It had to be expanding. In 1927,

THE MEANING OF THE HUBBLE CONSTANT

To understand the Hubble constant, think of the universe as a balloon with a number of spots on it being blown up at a steady rate. The distance between any two spots, randomly chosen, will increase as the balloon expands. The farther apart they are, the more the distance between them will increase every second. Since the balloon is being blown up at a steady rate, their relative speed will be proportional to their separation. That means the ratio between their speed and separation is a constant value. In the case of the universe, that value is the Hubble constant.

Belgian priest and physicist Georges Lemaître (1894–1966) published an article that connected Friedmann's ideas to Hubble's and Slipher's observations of redshifted galaxies.

THE HUBBLE CONSTANT AND THE AGE OF THE UNIVERSE

The Hubble constant is key in estimating both the age and size of the universe because it expresses the rate at which the universe is expanding. Hubble originally calculated the numeric value of H_0 to be about 100 miles per second (160 km per second) for every 1,000,000 light-years distance. Modern estimates, based on more precise measurements, now place that at about 15 mi/s (about 24 km/sec) per 1,000,000 light-years. Hubble therefore believed the universe to be some two to three billion years old. The best modern estimates by NASA place the occurrence of the big bang at 13.8 billion years ago.

THE COSMIC MICROWAVE BACKGROUND

Hubble's findings served as the basis for a growing knowledge of the cosmological model of the universe. There was, however, no further evidence to support the big bang theory beyond his original discovery of the expansion of the universe. Such proof would have to wait until technology caught up with theory. The technology finally came from the work of the American physicists Arno Penzias (1933–) and Robert Wilson (1936–) of the Bell Telephone Laboratories in New Jersey.

Bell Labs was a leader in communication technology, and in 1964, Penzias and Wilson were working on

ARNO PENZIAS *(LEFT)* AND ROBERT WILSON OF BELL TELEPHONE LABORATORIES IN NEW JERSEY WERE PIONEERS IN MICROWAVE COMMUNICATION TECHNOLOGY. IN 1964, THEY BUILT THE SUPER-SENSITIVE MICROWAVE RECEIVER SHOWN HERE, AND DISCOVERED AN UNCHANGING SIGNAL COMING FROM EVERY DIRECTION AT ALL TIMES AND SEASONS. THEY REALIZED IT WAS THE INTENSE GLOW OF THE BIG BANG THAT WAS REDSHIFTED SO MUCH THAT IT REACHED EARTH AS MICROWAVE ENERGY.

a system to communicate by microwaves, which are the part of the electromagnetic spectrum with wavelengths shorter than radio and television signals. The electromagnetic spectrum includes visible light, which has wavelengths ranging from roughly four hundred to eight hundred billionths of a meter, or ten to twenty billionths of an inch. Microwaves have much longer wavelengths, a few centimeters or inches.

Because signals spread out and get weaker, Penzias and Wilson needed to build sensitive receivers to detect them. Interference from other sources of microwaves would make it hard to receive messages. And no matter which direction they pointed their detector, they found low-level interference at one particular wavelength. Because it came from all directions, they first thought it was a problem with their antenna. Perhaps the solution was as simple as cleaning off accumulated bird droppings, but that didn't solve the problem.

The time of day or season of the year didn't change the level of noise either. It didn't matter that the Earth was continually changing its position through its rotation on its axis and orbit around the sun. This told them that the noise came from beyond even our solar system and galaxy. Otherwise, the noise would change as the Earth's movement pointed the detector in different directions.

Meanwhile, at New Jersey's Princeton University, two physicists, the American Robert H. Dicke (1916–1997) and Canadian James Peebles (1935–) were also looking at microwaves. Their work was based on a 1948 article by one of Friedmann's students, George Gamow (1904–1968), and Gamow's student Ralph Alpher (1921–2007), which was the first publication to calculate what the universe must have been like at time zero.

They didn't call it the big bang, but they realized the universe would have been super dense, incredibly hot, and glowing with electromagnetic radiation. For the first three hundred thousand years after that (a very short time compared to the age of the universe), the universe was full of electrically charged particles that would absorb that radiation. But then those charged particles began to form electrically neutral atoms, and the glow from the still very hot early universe could pass through space. Dicke and Peebles believed we should still be able to see that faraway glow that was only now reaching us from billions of light-years away.

But as Hubble's work had shown, the light from that glow would have such a large redshift that it would arrive in the form of microwaves, distributed evenly across the universe. Hearing of Dicke's and Peebles's work, Penzias and Wilson realized they had already found the radiation the two Princeton scientists sought.

In 1969, two British physicists and mathematicians, Sir Roger Penrose (1931–) and Stephen Hawking (1942–) gave the big bang theory additional support.

IN 1970, BRITISH MATHEMATICIANS AND PHYSICISTS ROGER PENROSE AND STEPHEN HAWKING *(SHOWN HERE)* PUBLISHED A PAPER THAT SUPPORTED THE BIG BANG THEORY IN AN UNEXPECTED WAY. PENROSE HAD DESCRIBED THE COLLAPSE OF A LARGE AMOUNT OF MATTER INTO A BLACK HOLE (A SMALL REGION OF SPACE THAT HAS SUCH HIGH DENSITY THAT NOT EVEN LIGHT CAN ESCAPE FROM ITS GRAVITY). HAWKING RECOGNIZED THAT TIME-REVERSING THAT COLLAPSE WOULD DESCRIBE THE BIG BANG. FROM 1979 TO 2009, HAWKING HELD THE PRESTIGIOUS LUCASIAN PROFESSORSHIP AT CAMBRIDGE UNIVERSITY, A POSITION OCCUPIED BY ISAAC NEWTON FROM 1669–1702.

Penrose had shown that a star that uses up its fuel begins to collapse under its own gravity. If the star is large enough, the collapse continues until it becomes so dense that the gravity at its surface does not even allow light to get out. The result was called a singularity and the area of space it inhabited was called a black hole. Hawking realized that if he reversed the direction of time in Penrose's theory, the collapse became an expansion, possibly mimicking the timeline of the big bang.

One of the most persuasive lines of evidence

in favor of the big bang came from computations of how much hydrogen and helium would have formed in the big bang, and then how much of the rest of the elements would have been created in early stars. The most famous result is called the B2FH paper, nicknamed after the initials of its authors, Margaret Burbidge (1919–), Geoffrey Burbidge (1925–2010), William A. Fowler (1911–1995), and Sir Fred Hoyle (1915–2001). Its actual title is "Synthesis of the Elements in Stars," and it was published in *Reviews of Modern Physics* in 1957. Its predictions matched actual measurements of the elements in stars so well that it was hard to consider any other explanation of how they came to be.

Ironically, the British astronomer Hoyle was a lifelong believer in the steady state theory of the universe. On a BBC radio broadcast in 1949, which was printed as a transcript in the April 1949 issue of the BBC magazine the *Listener*, Hoyle mocked Hubble's idea of an expanding universe that emerged from an explosion. "These theories were based on the hypothesis that all the matter in universe was created in one big bang at a particular time in the remote past." He used the phrase "big bang" as an insult, but it was so captivating that it actually helped popularize the theory. Now few scientists doubt that today's universe is the result of a big bang that happened many billions of years ago.

HUBBLE'S CELEBRITY AND LEGACY

The great observatory on Mount Wilson was only 1,600 miles (2,500 km) from the backyard in Missouri where Edwin Powell Hubble had first gazed at the wonders of the universe through his grandfather's telescope. Yet there was literally a universe of difference between what the two instruments could reveal. Still, the sense of awe that Hubble felt as a child could not have been more important to the man he had become.

He was open to new discoveries and questions. So his discovery of "island universes" transformed our view of the Earth's place in space and made him famous as the man who discovered galaxies and placed the solar system on a spiral arm of one such star system known as the Milky Way.

IN 1931, ALBERT EINSTEIN *(FRONT ROW, LEFT)* VISITED THE MOUNT WILSON OBSERVATORY, WHICH AT THAT TIME HOUSED THE WORLD'S LARGEST TELESCOPE. AMONG THE PEOPLE HE MET WAS EDWIN HUBBLE *(LEFT REAR)*, WHO HAD SHOWN TWO YEARS EARLIER THAT THE UNIVERSE WAS EXPANDING. BOTH MEN KNEW WHAT IT WAS LIKE TO BE CONSIDERED CELEBRITIES BECAUSE THEIR REVOLUTIONARY DISCOVERIES EXCITED THE GENERAL PUBLIC.

THE BENEFITS OF FAME

Hubble never expected to become acclaimed, but soon the influential and famous made their way to Mount Wilson to meet the man who had opened up the universe. His celebrity rose to even greater heights with the 1931 visit of Albert Einstein, who proclaimed that Hubble's work on the redshift of distant stars enabled him to eliminate the cosmological constant from his general theory of relativity. Einstein called the inclusion of that constant his "greatest blunder."

Hubble entertained scientists, politicians, and celebrities at both the observatory and with his wife, Grace, at his home in San Marino, California. Among their friends were some of the most famous names in entertainment, from composer Cole Porter to actor Gary Cooper. The couple—who never had any children—traveled extensively to deliver lectures on his work. He was the youngest person ever inducted into the National Academy of Sciences. Then in 1934 he received an honorary doctor of sciences from Oxford University in England, where he had earned his law degree in 1913.

Hubble was invited to deliver lectures both in America and abroad, meeting with the greatest scientific minds of his day everywhere he went. He published two popular books, *The Realm of the Nebulae* (1936) and *The Observational Approach to Cosmology* (1937), both based on his lectures delivered at Yale University and elsewhere.

BACK TO WAR

When America again went to war in 1941, following the Japanese bombing of the Pearl Harbor Naval Base in Hawaii, Hubble responded as he had to his country's entry into World War I: he applied for a job in the military.

Now fifty-two years old and one of the country's most famous scientists, he was made head of the ballistics research program at Maryland's Aberdeen Proving Ground. The work at Aberdeen was as different as possible from the quiet research of observing the heavens through a telescopic site. It involved the science of ballistics, or the motion of projectiles such as bullets and bombs. Ammunition of all sorts was tested and studied to learn how to make the most efficient weapons for the war against the Axis powers (Germany, Italy, Japan, and their allies).

Edwin and Grace Hubble were uprooted from their normal academic lives and far from home. He was happy to do his part to restore world peace, but as the war neared its end with America and its allies on the road to victory, he became anxious to get back to California and his real work, astronomy.

THE HALE TELESCOPE

After the war, the Hubbles returned to Caltech. In addition to his regular work at the 100-inch (254-cm)

Mount Wilson telescope, Edwin Hubble had been involved in the development of an even larger instrument for Caltech: the Hale Telescope, named after his professor and colleague, George Ellery Hale, which was to be located atop nearby Palomar Mountain.

The telescope had been in the works since 1928. Its 200-inch (508-cm), 20-ton Pyrex glass disk mirror was cast at the Corning Glass Works in New York and shipped to Pasadena in 1935 for the long and delicate process of grinding and polishing. The building that was to house this great telescope had moving parts that weighed some 530 tons (481 metric tons) and featured a 1,000-ton (907 metric ton) rotating dome. World War II interrupted the polishing of the mirror. It was finally completed and installed into

HUBBLE'S LAST GREAT PROJECT WAS THE DESIGN AND DEVELOPMENT OF THE HALE TELESCOPE, NAMED AFTER HIS COLLEAGUE AND PROFESSOR GEORGE ELLERY HALE, ON PALOMAR MOUNTAIN, WHICH WAS DEDICATED IN 1948. HUBBLE LAST USED IT ON SEPTEMBER 1, 1953, 27 DAYS BEFORE HIS DEATH. FOR MANY YEARS, ITS 200-INCH (508-CM) DIAMETER MIRROR MADE IT THE LARGEST IN THE WORLD, AND IT REMAINS ONE OF THE WORLD'S GREATEST ASTRONOMICAL INSTRUMENTS. THIS PHOTO FROM 2008 SHOWS ITS NEW LASER ADAPTIVE OPTICS SYSTEM IN OPERATION. THE LASER CREATES AN ARTIFICIAL STAR, WHICH ENABLES THE OPTICAL SYSTEM TO AUTOMATICALLY CORRECT ITSELF FOR ATMOSPHERIC DISTORTION, KNOWN AS TWINKLING.

the 55-foot (17-meter) long barrel of the telescope in November 1947.

The Hale Telescope was dedicated on June 3, 1948. The opening was so momentous that the United States Postal Service created the world's first "space stamp," a 3-cent first-class stamp issued August 30, 1948. Edwin Hubble was given the honor of processing the first photographic plate, which was saved for posterity. The plate is of a variable nebula and bears his initials.

When technological problems caused a delay in further observations through the Hale, the Hubbles used the time to travel back to England for more lectures and his election as an honorary fellow of Oxford University's Queen's College. In July 1949, while on vacation in Colorado, Hubble experienced a heart attack. A second attack followed several days later.

Hubble eventually recovered sufficiently to return to work, but always with Grace watching carefully over him. He continued on a modified work and travel schedule, making one final trip to England in April 1953 to address the Royal Astronomical Society and meet the young Queen Elizabeth II.

Hubble made his last visit to Palomar Mountain on September 1, 1953, spending several hours over the course of three nights viewing the heavens through the great telescope. On September 28, as he was returning home with Grace, Edwin Powell Hubble passed out in the car. He had suffered a fatal stroke.

THE HUBBLE SPACE TELESCOPE

Edwin Hubble's legacy in the world of astronomy and physics has proved to be vast and undeniable. His observations of spiral nebulae and measurement of their distances awoke the world to the true vastness of the universe. His name has been attached to many scientific concepts. Perhaps most well known to the world beyond the astronomical community and the most fitting tribute to him is the Hubble Space Telescope (HST).

Launched on April 25, 1990, by the space shuttle

THE HUBBLE SPACE TELESCOPE (HST), SEEN HERE IN AN ENVIRONMENTAL CHAMBER WHERE IT WAS TESTED UNDER CONDITIONS SIMULATING THOSE IT WOULD ENCOUNTER IN SPACE, WAS SUCCESSFULLY LAUNCHED ON APRIL 24, 1990. IT HAS PRODUCED A LARGE COLLECTION OF SPECTACULAR IMAGES FROM SOLAR SYSTEM OBJECTS TO THE MOST DISTANT GALAXIES. IT HAS HAD FOUR MAINTENANCE AND UPGRADE MISSIONS BY SPACE SHUTTLE ASTRONAUTS, THE LAST IN 2009. WITH THE RETIREMENT OF THE SPACE SHUTTLE FLEET, HST IS EXPECTED TO OPERATE UNTIL AT LEAST 2015.

Discovery, the 12.5-ton (13.3 metric ton) HST orbits 370 miles (595 km) over the Earth, far above the distorting effects of the planet's atmosphere. Unlike Earth-based telescopes, the Hubble is not restricted to operation at night or only during clear weather. Its powerful and precise instruments provide stunning views of the farthest reaches of the universe twenty-four hours a day. It sees billions of light-years farther into space than was ever thought possible during Hubble's time. With it, scientists can view galaxies as they were during earlier stages of the universe's existence, peering deeper into space and farther back into time than even Hubble had ever imagined.

All telescopes must eventually be retired, and that fact of life is even more an issue when maintenance sometimes requires a visit by astronauts. In May 2009, as the space shuttle program was nearing its end, astronauts upgraded the HST one more time. It immediately began sending better images than ever before and was expected to continue to do so until at least 2015.

By that time, many of the HST's functions are scheduled to be taken over by other space telescopes and newer ground-based telescopes using improved technology called adaptive optics that eliminates much of the atmospheric distortion in the visible region. The scheduled launch of the James Webb Space Telescope in 2018 will replace some of the HST's functions.

FOR GALAXIES BILLIONS OF LIGHT YEARS AWAY, ASTRONOMERS USE A "STANDARD CANDLE" CALLED A TYPE 1A SUPERNOVA, WHICH RELEASES A PRECISELY KNOWN AMOUNT OF ENERGY WHEN IT EXPLODES. THIS IMAGE SHOWS WHAT REMAINS OF SUCH A SUPERNOVA IN A NEARBY DWARF GALAXY THAT WOULD HAVE BEEN VISIBLE ON EARTH WITHOUT A TELESCOPE ABOUT FOUR HUNDRED YEARS AGO. IT HAS SINCE SPREAD OUT OVER TWENTY-THREE LIGHT-YEARS. THE PINK EDGE IS THE SHOCK WAVE (LIKE A SONIC BOOM FOR LIGHT) AT ITS OUTER EDGE. THE GREEN AND BLUE AREA IS GAS BEING HEATED BY X-RAYS. THE PHOTO OF THE BACKGROUND STAR FIELD WAS PRODUCED BY THE HUBBLE SPACE TELESCOPE. THE SUPERNOVA REMNANT WAS PHOTOGRAPHED BY THE CHANDRA X-RAY OBSERVATORY.

THE ACCELERATING UNIVERSE AND DARK ENERGY

Progress in science never stops. And sometimes, revolutionary breakthroughs are replaced by other breakthroughs later. That is true of the Hubble constant. As astronomy advanced, telescopes began observing more and more distant parts of the universe.

At a certain distance, Cepheid variables are too dim and redshifted to see. Fortunately, astronomers found that they could use another much brighter but rarer type of star called a Type 1a supernova to measure distances. A supernova occurs when a star explodes. There are several types of supernova, and most vary in brightness. But all Type 1a supernovae release the same amount of energy when they explode. And they are bright enough to be seen at the farthest distances across the universe.

In the late twentieth and early twenty-first centuries, scientists measuring distant galaxies using Type 1a supernova explosions discovered that Hubble's law

STANDARD CANDLES FOR DISTANT GALAXIES

A type 1a supernova is an exploding white dwarf star that is part of a double star system. It starts out smaller than 1.44 times as massive as the sun. As time passes, the gravity of the white dwarf draws away some of its partner's outer material. It grows until its mass reaches the critical amount (called the Chandrasekhar limit). At that point it explodes into a Type 1a supernova.

Since scientists always know how much mass and energy a Type 1a supernova has, they can measure its distance by its apparent brightness. That makes it an excellent "standard candle" for very distant galaxies.

was not quite correct. The redshifts of the most distant galaxies, including many studied by the Advanced Camera for Surveys that was added to the HST when astronauts serviced in it 2002, were even greater than expected. Instead of showing a universe that was expanding like a balloon being blown up at a steady rate, the new evidence showed that the expansion was speeding up, as if gravity were acting in reverse.

As the evidence grew that their measurements were correct, scientists began calling this odd phenomenon dark energy. The discovery was so important it won the 2011 Nobel Prize in Physics. Although it is still not clear where dark energy is coming from, perhaps the best explanation is that it is caused by Einstein's cosmological constant.

So if Albert Einstein were alive today, he would no longer call the cosmological constant a blunder. Instead, it would be another puzzle to be solved. And if Edwin Hubble were still alive, he would not be disappointed that his law was proving not to be exactly correct. He would view it in the same way as he viewed Vesto Slipher's discovery of large redshifts in spiral nebulae, as a surprising and unexplained phenomenon that is worth looking into further.

That's the way revolutionary thinkers view the universe. And that's why they leave behind a legacy of discovery for the rest of us to build on.

1889: Edwin Powell Hubble is born on November 20 in Marshfield, Missouri.

1897: Hubble has his first look through a telescope at his grandfather's house.

1905: Albert Einstein publishes his special theory of relativity.

1906: Hubble graduates high school in Wheaton, Illinois, and enters the University of Chicago.

1910: Hubble wins a scholarship to study in England. He studies law for three years at Oxford University.

1912: Henrietta Swan Leavitt publishes her discovery of a relationship between the luminosity and period of Cepheid variable stars.

1914: Hubble decides to return to the study of astronomy at the University of Chicago. In August he is elected a member of the American Astronomical Society.

1915: Albert Einstein publishes his general theory of relativity.

1917: Hubble receives his doctorate and joins the United States Army, where he achieves the rank of major.

1918: Using Cepheid variables, Harlow Shapley determines the size of the Milky Way galaxy.

1919: Hubble leaves the army and returns to the United States, where he accepts a position at California's Mount Wilson Observatory. Two teams of observers viewing a solar eclipse show that the predictions of general relativity are valid.

1922: Alexander Friedmann publishes a paper on general relativity that includes the theoretical prediction of an expanding universe.

1923: Hubble discovers a Cepheid variable star in the Andromeda nebula.

1924: Hubble marries Grace Burke Leib on February 26. On November 25, an article in the *New York Times* reveals Hubble's discovery of "island universes."

1926: Hubble publishes his classification of galaxies in the *Astrophysical Journal*.

1927: Georges Lemaître publishes a paper that connects Friedmann's idea to the observation of redshifted galaxies

1929: Hubble publishes "A Relation Between Distance and Radial Velocity Among Extra-Galactic Nebulae" in the *Proceedings of the National Academy of Sciences*. It includes what has become known as Hubble's law, which describes a universe that is expanding at a steady rate.

1936: Hubble publishes his book *The Realm of the Nebulae*.

1937: Hubble publishes his book *The Observational Approach to Cosmology*.

1942: Hubble is asked to head up the ballistics research program at Maryland's Aberdeen Proving Ground.

1948: Alpher and Gamow publish the first paper to describe the big bang, although they did not use the term.

1949: Fred Hoyle first uses the term "big bang" to mock the idea of an expanding universe. It became so popular that it has become the name of the theory.

1953: Hubble dies on September 28.

1957: The famous B2FH paper predicts how much hydrogen and helium would have been produced by the big bang. The predictions matched observations.

1965: Robert Wilson and Arno Penzias of Bell Telephone Laboratories discover the mysterious microwave "background noise" that Princeton University physicists Robert H. Dicke and James Peebles later determine to be a remnant of the big bang.

1969: Roger Penrose and Stephen W. Hawking realize that their theoretical work on black holes supports the big bang.

1990: The Hubble Space Telescope (HST) is launched aboard the space shuttle *Discovery* on April 25.

2002: Astronauts perform HST servicing mission 3B, including the addition of the Advanced Camera for Surveys. That camera studied Type 1a supernovas of very distant galaxies and confirmed that the expansion of the universe is speeding up. This phenomenon is called dark energy.

2009: Final servicing mission extends the life of the HST until approximately 2015.

2011: Nobel Prize in Physics awarded for the discovery of dark energy.

ASTRONOMER A person who studies distant objects and events outside the Earth's atmosphere, such as the sun, moon, planets, stars, galaxies, and other objects in the solar system and beyond.

BLACK HOLE A collapsed star with such strong gravity that not even light can escape.

BLUESHIFT The shortening of the wavelength of light caused by the movement of the source toward the observer, thus shifting the color toward the blue end of the visible spectrum.

CELESTIAL Of or relating to the sky.

CEPHEID VARIABLE A type of star, first seen in the constellation Cepheus, whose apparent brightness varies periodically at a rate that is related to its absolute brightness in a predictable way.

COSMOLOGICAL CONSTANT A quantity that Einstein added to his general theory of relativity so that an unchanging universe would be possible but is now suspected to be the source of dark energy.

COSMOLOGY The study of the large-scale structure and evolution of the universe.

DARK ENERGY A phenomenon that is causing the expansion of the universe to speed up.

DEFERENT A circle centered on the point halfway between Earth and the equant, used in Ptolemy's geocentric description of the universe as a planet's main motion.

DOPPLER EFFECT The change in length of a wave caused by the relative motion of the source toward or away from an observer. It was originally observed in sound waves, but it also applies to light where it is called a red shift or blue shift.

ELLIPSE A particular type of an oval that corresponds to the shape of the orbit of a planet or a comet that returns periodically.

EPICYCLE A circle around a point on the deferent, used to explain the paths of the sun, moon, and planets in Ptolemy's geocentric description of the universe.

EQUANT A point used in Ptolemy's geocentric description of the universe to explain the sun's changing speed around Earth at different times of the year. He stated that the sun changed the angle it made with the line between the equant and Earth at a constant rate.

FREQUENCY The number of complete oscillations, or waves, per second for an electromagnetic wave.

GALAXY A large body of gas, dust, stars, and their planets, held together by their mutual gravitational attraction.

GEOCENTRIC MODEL A description of the universe with the earth at the center and all other objects moving around it.

HELIOCENTRIC MODEL A description of the universe with the sun at the center and all other objects moving around it.

LIGHT-YEAR The distance that light travels in one year, equaling 5.88 trillion miles (9.46 trillion km).

LUMINOSITY A measurement of the rate that a star produces energy.

MICROWAVE A type of electromagnetic wave with a wavelength in the range between a millimeter and a meter.

NEBULA An object that appears to be a cloudlike structure in space. It can be gas or dust in our galaxy or another galaxy so far away that it looks like a spiral cloud.

PARALLAX The apparent change in location of an object against a background caused by the change in position of the observer.

REDSHIFT The lengthening of the wavelength of light caused by the movement of the source away from the observer, thus shifting the color toward the red end of the visible spectrum.

SPECTRUM The set of wavelengths contained in a beam of light or other type of wave.

STANDARD CANDLE A bright celestial object whose absolute luminosity can be determined by another property, such as the period of variation of a Cepheid variable or the explosion of a Type 1a supernova.

TYPE 1A SUPERNOVA A very bright explosion that results when a white dwarf in a double star system reaches a certain mass by drawing matter from its companion star.

FOR MORE INFORMATION

American Astronomical Society (AAS)

2000 Florida Avenue NW, Suite 400

Washington, DC 20009-1231

(202) 328-2010

Web site: http://www.aas.org

The mission of the AAS is to enhance and share humanity's scientific understanding of the universe. It sponsors meetings and publishes journals for scientists and also publishes information for the public, educators, and people interested in careers in astronomy.

American Institute of Physics (AIP)

One Physics Ellipse

College Park, MD 20740-3843

(301) 209-3100

Web site: http://www.aip.org

The American Institute of Physics is the umbrella organization for many different professional societies of physical scientists. It publishes numerous journals for scientists and magazines for educators, the public, and students interested in careers in physics. Its Center for the History of Physics contains a library and archive of historical books and photographs. The AIP Web site includes a link to the center with a large number of online articles and images, including a discussion of how science came to understand planetary motion.

Mount Wilson Observatory

466 Foothill Boulevard, #327

La Canada, CA 91011

(626) 440-9016

Web site: http://www.mtwilson.edu

The observatory where Edwin Hubble did much of his work is still an important scientific facility.

Royal Astronomical Society of Canada (RASC)

203-4920 Dundas Street West

Toronto, ON M9A 1B7

Canada

(888) 924-7272 (in Canada); 416-924-7973

Web site: http://www.rasc.ca

The Royal Astronomical Society of Canada is Canada's leading astronomy organization. It aims to inspire curiosity in all Canadians about the universe, to share scientific knowledge, and to foster under-standing of astronomy for all through activities including education, research, and community outreach activities. Its publications and its extensive Web site have materials for scientists, researchers, teachers, and students of all ages.

Space Telescope Science Institute (STScI)

Office of Public Outreach

3700 San Martin Drive

Baltimore, MD 21218

(410) 338-4444

Web site: http://www.hubblesite.org

The Space Telescope Science Institute is the organization that operates the Hubble Space Telescope and plans for future observatories in space. The Hubble Web site states, "At the Space Telescope Science Institute (STScI), we're working hard to study and explain the once-unimaginable celestial phenomena now made visible using Hubble's cutting-edge technology. In the course of this exploration we will continue to share with you the grace and beauty of the universe, because the discoveries belong to all of us."

Yerkes Observatory

373 W. Geneva Street

Williams Bay, WI 53191

(262) 245-5555

Web site: http://astro.uchicago.edu/yerkes

The Web site calls the Yerkes Observatory "the birth-place of modern astrophysics," and adds, "Until the mid-1960's, Yerkes Observatory housed all of the department's activities. Today the 77-acre [31 hectare], park-like site in southeast Wisconsin provides laboratory space and access to telescopes for research and instruction." Tours and educational activities are available.

WEB SITES

Due to the changing nature of Internet links, the Rosen Publishing Group has developed an online list of Web sites related to the subject of this book. This site is updated regularly. Please use this link to access the list:

http://www.rosenlinks.com/RDSP/hubble

FOR FURTHER READING

Anderson, Michael. *Pioneers in Astronomy and Space Exploration*. New York, NY: Britannica Educational Publishing, 2013.

Aughton, Peter. *The Story of Astronomy: From Babylonian Stargazers to the Search for the Big Bang*. London, England: Quercus, 2008.

Bartusiak, Marcia. *The Day We Found the Universe*. New York, NY: Pantheon Books, 2009.

Bortz, Fred. *Seven Wonders of Space Technology*. Minneapolis, MN: Twenty-First Century Books, 2011.

Boss, Alan. *The Crowded Universe: The Search for Living Planets*. New York, NY: Basic Books, 2009.

Curley, Robert. *Scientists and Inventors of the Universe*. New York, NY: Britannica Educational Publishing, 2013.

Dyson, Marianne. *Astronomy: Decade by Decade* (Twentieth Century Science). New York, NY: Facts On File, 2007.

Jankowski, Connie. *Astronomers: From Copernicus to Crisp*. Mankato, MN: Compass Point Books, 2009.

Miller, Ron. *Recentering the Universe: The Radical Theories of Copernicus, Kepler, and Galileo*. Minneapolis, MN: Twenty-First Century Books, 2014.

Moore, Patrick. *Men of the Stars*. New York, NY: Gallery Books, 1986.

Moore, Patrick, and Leif Robinson. *Astronomy Encyclopedia*. Oxford, England: Oxford University Press Children's Books, 2002.

Perricone, Mike. *The Big Bang*. New York, NY: Chelsea House Publishers, 2009.

Robinson, Andrew, ed. *The Scientists: An Epic of Discovery*. New York, NY: Thames and Hudson, 2012.

Timmons, Todd. *Makers of Western Science: The Works and Words of 24 Visionaries from Copernicus to Watson and Crick*. Jefferson, NC: McFarland & Co., 2012

Wilkins, Jamie, and Robert Dunn. *300 Astronomical Objects: A Visual Reference to the Universe*. Richmond Hill, VA: Firefly Books, 2011.

Woolfson, M. M. *Time, Space, Stars, & Man: The Story of the Big Bang*. Hackensack, NJ: Imperial College Press, 2012.

BIBLIOGRAPHY

Belenkiy, Ari. "Alexander Friedmann and the Origins of Modern Cosmology." *Physics Today*. Retrieved March 18, 2013 (http://dx.doi.org/10.1063/PT.3.1750).

Camp, Carole Ann. *American Astronomers, Searchers and Wonderers*. Springfield, NJ: Enslow Publishers, 1995.

Center for the History of Physics, American Institute of Physics. "Big Bang or Steady State? Creation of the Elements, Ideas of Cosmology." Retrieved March 18, 2013 (http://www.aip.org/history/cosmology/ideas/bigbang.htm Retrieved March 18, 2013).

Christianson, Gale E. *Edwin Hubble: Mariner of the Nebulae*. Toronto, ON, Canada: University of Chicago Press, 1996.

Fox, Mary Virginia. *Edwin Hubble, American Astronomer*. New York, NY: Franklin Watts, 1997.

Hawking, Stephen. *A Brief History of Time: The Updated and Expanded Tenth Anniversary Edition*. New York, NY: Bantam, 1998.

Hubblesite. "Dark Energy." Retrieved March 18, 2013 (http://hubblesite.org/hubble_discoveries/dark_energy/).

Huchra, John P. "The Hubble Constant." Harvard-Smithsonian Center, 2008. Retrieved March 18, 2013 (https://www.cfa.harvard.edu/~dfabricant/huchra/hubble).

Iz quotes. From BBC magazine the *Listener*, April 1949. Retrieved March 18, 2013 Retrieved March 18, 2013 (http://izquotes.com/quote/238941).

Kant, Immanuel (translated by Ian Johnson, Vancouver Island University). "Universal Natural History and Theory of the Heavens, or An Essay on the Constitution and the Mechanical Origin of the Entire Structure of the Universe Based on Newtonian Principles." Retrieved March 18, 2013 (http://www .calstatela.edu/faculty/kaniol/a360/Kant.Island .Universe.Theory.htm).

Maran, Stephen P. *Astronomy for Dummies*. New York, NY: IDG Books, 1999.

Ryden, Barbara. *Introduction to Cosmology*. Boston, MA: Addison-Wesley, 2002.

Zannos, Susan. *Edwin Hubble and the Theory of the Expanding Universe* (Unlocking the Secrets of Science). Hockessin, DE: Mitchell Lane, 2003.

INDEX

ABOUT THE AUTHOR

After earning his Ph.D. at Carnegie Mellon University in 1971, physicist Fred Bortz set off on an interesting and varied twenty-five-year career in teaching and research. From 1979 to 1994, he was on staff at Carnegie Mellon, where his work evolved from research to outreach.

After his third book, *Catastrophe!: Great Engineering Failure—and Success*, was designated a "Selector's Choice" on the 1996 list of Outstanding Science Trade Books for Children, he decided to spend the rest of his career as a full-time writer. His books, now numbering nearly thirty, have since won awards, including the American Institute of Physics Science Writing Award, and recognition on several best books lists.

Known on the Internet as the smiling, bowtie-wearing Dr. Fred, he welcomes inquisitive visitors to his Web site at www.fredbortz.com.

PHOTO CREDITS